DON'T JUDGE A BOOK BY ITS COVER

REGINALD PAUL

Don't Judge A Book By It's Cover

By Reginald Paul

Don't Judge a Book By Its Cover
By Reginald Paul

Published by Trient Press, *Don't Judge a Book By Its Cover* explores the complexities of human perception and the importance of seeing beyond appearances. Through thoughtful analysis and real-life examples, Reginald Paul challenges readers to reconsider their assumptions and embrace a deeper understanding of those around them.

Publisher Information
Trient Press

5470 Kietzke Lane Suite 300 - #394
Reno, NV 89511
Phone: (775) 249-7401
Website: www.trientpress.com

ISBN
eBook: 979-8-88990-211-9
Paperback: 979-8-88990-212-6

All rights reserved.
Trient Press, an imprint of Trient Press.

First Trient Press mass market printing: September 2025.
Trient Press is a registered trademark.

Printed in the USA.

~CONTENTS~

Introduction 4
Let Your Friend Know 6
Judging A Book By It's Cover 8
Storms 10
Let It Go 12
Change Your Atmosphere 14
Changing Your Atmosphere 16
You've Got To Believe 18
Don't Control What You Cannot 20
The Grind 22
Naysayers 24
Be You 26
Use Your Time Wisely 28
Step Out Of Your Comfort Zone 30
Stepping Out Of Your Comfort Zone 32
Get Ready 34
Stay Focused 36
Staying Focused 38
Is Adversity Needed? 40
Overcoming Adversity 42
Open Your Gift 44
Overcoming The Odds 46
Don't Lie To Yourself 48
Epilogue 50
About The Author 51

~INTRODUCTION~

There are only two things you can do if you're in a situation you dislike: continue to tolerate it or do something about it. The degree to which we can do something varies, of course, but whether we do something or not is entirely up to us. I was often judged because of the color of my skin and faced discrimination at every stop in life where another decision-maker could help me or block me. Through my experiences, I learned that people don't usually go even the slightest bit further to see who you are. They only interface with an image of you they have in their minds.

I also learned that taking the maximum responsibility for one's own life is by far the best decision one can make. The fewer decision-makers there are tied to your fulfillment, the happier you can be. But it is true that regardless of how self-sufficient you become, you will always have to interface with others for your success. Even at the height of his success, Steve Jobs was beholden to his board. And for that, I have developed a philosophy of being so good that they can't afford to misjudge you.

We know that the racial discrimination problem in America is far from gone, but Barack Obama was so competent and charismatic that a majority of the country was forced to see past normalized stereotypes and accept him not just as a leader but as the president of the united states.

In this book, you will find my core appeal to stop judging people by aspects of their appearance that they cannot control. More importantly, you'll learn how you can weather the storms of life by working on yourself and excelling at the best you have to offer. Finally, you will learn how you can carry yourself with authenticity, so the people who lean towards judging things by their appearances are forced to rethink their prejudices.

This is a book for people who have been in my position. People who feel boxed into categories and labels they don't identify with, people who are stereotyped, and people who feel like their appearance is getting in the way of their success. If you are one of them, let me tell you: you can become a multimillionaire, even a multimillionaire, despite people's views on your appearance. You must be so good; they can't afford to stay judgmental.

~LET YOUR FRIEND KNOW~

Picture this, you are in a room, and there's a fire in the one next to it. What do you do? Of course, the moment you get a hint of danger, you leap into action. You either collect what's precious to you and escape or try to manage the condition. Either way, you're super-focused on the problem. During such times, we don't remember our blessings. I would like to tell you that in the situation I just presented, there's a hidden blessing: your ability to smell. The fact that you can sniff out smoke (or have a smoke detector) is what keeps you out of trouble. It isn't pleasant to take in the smell of smoke, but you sure are glad you got alerted on time.

If your smoke detector didn't go off, it would save you from that moment of panic but only for a while before things get out of control and become obvious anyway.

And then you panic a lot more. In my opinion, you are, among other things, a smoke detector to your friends' mistakes. But too many people are bound by an unspoken pact of protecting their friends' feelings. If your job description as a friend is to always agree with your friend, you've gotten yourself into a bad deal. Signing up to be someone's friend only to protect their feelings is like taking a job as a captain of a sinking ship. Even if you do the best job, you still will get less than ideal results.

So what should you do? Let your friend know if you care about them more than you care about feeling like a good friend. Being a good friend or a good family member may not always correspond with feeling like one. It might seem more "Friendly" to say "you're right" or "that's a good choice" to someone, but authenticity is the best gift you can give to someone you care about.

When you protect someone's feelings, you assume they're too weak to face reality, but when you let them know what you really think, you give them the highest compliment: that they are tough enough to handle the truth.

Let's look at what happens if you shy away from this choice: you've saved yourself from feeling bad, but your friend has to face the consequences of their bad decisions. Whatever comes from their decisions is on your conscience. Of course, anything taken to an extreme will inevitably become problematic. So while I encourage you to be honest with your friends, I implore you to do so with care. You cannot force your opinion on them. It is possible that your opinion is wrong. So, simply fulfill your duty to voice your opinion and make your best case for why they need to change their mind. If you don't, then you shoulder the burden of whatever destruction comes your friends' way.

~JUDGING A BOOK BY ITS COVER~

Everyone says, "don't judge a book by its cover." Almost no one practices that. Humans are wired to judge things by their appearance because it is the least time-consuming way to build patterns. If you tip someone because they served you dinner while wearing a server's uniform, you judged them by their appearance. We must first understand that the repetitive proclamations of not judging a book by its cover does not free you of the responsibility to carry yourself in congruence with your goals and true worth.

There are some people who will judge you based on aspects of your appearance that you cannot change. Pleasing them is not your duty. But you control your body language, your facial expressions, and what you wear. And it is your duty to excel in each of those aspects to the point that people respect you at first glance.

Some people might misconstrue this as permission or encouragement to be fake. If you actually try to fake your appearance, it shows. People can sniff it from a mile away and know you're inauthentic. What I am saying is that you have to put effort into your appearance, so it matches your internal reality. Your appearance doesn't automatically reflect your true worth.

If you're an entrepreneur who wants to build a multi-million dollar business, but you are being underestimated, you shouldn't dress like someone who daydreams about becoming a millionaire. Dress like someone who knows he is going to be a millionaire soon. Most of us adopt the character we get boxed into. Walk the path that's meant for you.

What others say matters a lot when your self-worth comes from them. Self-worth is crucial, and people go to great lengths to feel worthy. If your sense of value is tied to others' opinions, you will always look at them to tell you who you are. But if you know who you are, what others think doesn't matter. Raise your self-esteem by doing things that will earn your own respect.

Once you respect yourself, you won't seek it from others, especially not superficial people. Finally, I want to emphasize that walking to your own beat does not mean that you don't care about others. You should not care about what they think of you, but you should always have compassion for others. If you take your freedom from their opinions as a license to do whatever you want, including bad things, I warn you that the universe will balance things out. Do good and be good but don't falsify your authenticity to appear good. As long as you know what you're doing is right, you will sleep well at night.

~STORMS~

Earlier in this book, I used the analogy of fire to convey the importance of early detection. Now I want to explore how you can approach problems you can see on the horizon. I see issues one can't control as storms. When you see a storm is coming, you can't do anything to stop the storm, but that doesn't mean you have to sit and take as much damage as possible.

In life, people can get complacent when they see an issue coming a mile away. An example of this would be a black youth applying for a job. It is likely (to varying degrees) that the employer may have a certain perception of the candidate because of the color of their skin. That prejudice is the storm. The person who shows up with a pessimistic outlook expecting to get rejected due to racial prejudice is like a man who observes a storm brewing but stays put.

On the other hand, the man who dresses up well, and shows up for the interview in a way that everything about him breaks racial stereotypes and forces the general public to reconsider what they think of black men in general, is like the man who sees a storm coming and has a bunker ready by the time it hits.

The first step, however, is to be willing to see reality as it is. Just like with the fire analogy, you need detection to manage the situation. And that's why you must surround yourself with people unafraid to give you a reality check.

If you rely only on your perception, you wouldn't know the kind of damage a storm would do even if you found out about its approach early on. That puts you at a disadvantage in terms of preparation and reinforcement. Let's suppose you see a storm coming, and you decide to build an underground bunker. You feel like it is a great idea, and all your friends are calling you a genius. This, of course, feels good.

But then a friend protests. He says it is a bad idea because your city is below sea-level and there's an ocean around. The storm, he asserts, can become a tsunami, and water can flood the bunker. Cherish that friend because he is willing to sacrifice temporary comradery and bear the weight of your anger just to introduce you to a new perspective. When preparing for storms, cherish every perspective and especially ones that aren't yours. And then make your decision and stick to it.

~LET IT GO~

You must learn to tell the difference between a wire and a barbed wire. So many people hold on to burning ropes that char their hands, and it isn't even pragmatic. Holding onto a hot wire if you're hanging from a cliff might make sense. However, more people are holding onto a burning rope while hanging from 6 feet above the ground with a trampoline underneath. The only reason they don't let go is that they have exaggerated the consequences of letting go. Let it go; you'll be fine.

People don't realize the concept of opportunity cost. Let's suppose you had a hundred dollars, and some guy came up to you offering you a baseball card for your money, and you bought it. Would you be happy if you sold it for 150 dollars? Of course. But you would be miserable if you learned that the same card sold for a million dollars two years later.

That is the opportunity cost of choosing cash at $150 over possession of the card. It works in reverse as well. And for the topic at hand, this is much more relevant. Imagine you have a property worth a million dollars. But tomorrow, it will go down in value by one dollar. The next, it will go down by two, and by the third, it will go down by double that; four dollars. How long would you hold onto the property?

When I ask people this, they typically say they'll hold it for a couple of months while they get their affairs in order. And then look for a buyer. But guess what, a dollar doubled every day becomes $536870912 by day thirty. In other words, by day 21, you would have lost over a million dollars making what you held onto worthless.

People do not understand the destructive power of holding onto things they shouldn't hold onto. And the longer you keep grabbing what you're not supposed to, the costlier it becomes. So why do people do it? Because they're afraid. They don't know what to do after letting go. As a result, they hold on with nothing more than hope that somehow the laws of the universe will change.

Some hold on to jobs; others hold on to toxic friendships. And then some hold onto grudges. Yes, even that can be destructive. Why? Because the focus and emotional energy that goes into holding onto animosity could be going towards achieving your dreams.

~CHANGE YOUR ATMOSPHERE~

I firmly believe that if you've stayed in the same place for a long time, it is time to change your atmosphere. This is critical in the physical sense as much as it is in the metaphysical sense. It is a bit of a Mexican standoff, I must admit: in certain spaces, you can't transform your mind because of your environment, but you can't dare to change your environment because of your current mindset.

So what do you do with this stalemate? What should you change first? I would advise you to change your mind first. Many coaches and speakers push the idea of changing one's mind, but that is only a temporary solution. It is possible to change your mind temporarily in a rigid environment but sooner or later, you fall back into your old patterns. The trick, therefore, is to change your mind and while you are in an open-minded state, take the practical step of changing your environment.

As a result, you will be in a different space where you can afford to stay in a different head space. Procrastination is among the top reasons people don't succeed. But procrastination goes hand in hand with comfort. And when you get comfortable in a loop, you stop growing. So please pay attention even if you're "okay" with your environment.

In fact, you should pay more attention to this chapter if you're "fine" with being where you are. People who know they don't like their environment will eventually reach a breaking point and make a change. But those who convince themselves that they're fine are the ones who miss out on all the benefits of changing their environment.

Often, you need to step away to step up. I was in an environment where stepping up meant getting in more trouble with the law. Had I excelled in that, I would be in a different place than I am now that I've excelled in a different area. Of course, I didn't have the luxury of reading this book or having a mentor caution me against complacency in a toxic environment.

For better or worse, I got a reality check when I faced jail-time as a 14-year-old. This opened my eyes, and I asked myself one question that changed everything: do you want to commit crimes and gamble everything you have? And because I answered that with "no," I have two college degrees. I had challenges sticking to the plan. Certain factors are outside your control, with how others judge you being a chief one. And as a result, I had two felony charges as an adult but didn't let them hinder me. Had I stayed in the same environment, those felonies would have become a right of passage into more crime. So ultimately, it was all a matter of changing the internal and external atmosphere.

~CHANGING YOUR ATMOSPHERE~

Now that we have discussed the importance of change in one's atmosphere let's look at a recent example of change. As I am writing this book, the world is facing COVID-19, and it is forcing us to change. The initial lock-downs came as a reality check as most people were forced to sit down and have a conversation with themselves. With nothing to distract us, we got to face our thoughts and feelings. Many of us decided that it was time to change.

Whether you're reading this while the COVID crisis is keeping us indoors, or you're reading this a decade from now when things have gotten normal: always make time for reflection. You don't always need a lock-down to sit and think about your situation and the future prospects. This self-dialogue can guide you towards fruitful change.

During Covid-19 lock-downs, many people see their past situations as better than their present, but if you truly set your mind to the right tasks, you can create a future where you're better off for going through the lock-downs. In any situation in life, you can ask yourself, "What should I do so that my disadvantage becomes my asset?" And once you find out what that thing is, you can give it your best shot.

I would also urge you to be thankful for every disruption. Because without disruption, you can fall into a habitual pattern. What you did to get where you are isn't going to get you any further. You need to change your patterns to fit your new goals. People lost their well-deserved jobs during COVID, but many of them are starting their own businesses and working for themselves as I write this.

This moment is an empowering one for millions choosing to take things into their own hands and a dis-empowering one for those waiting for life to go back to as it was. Between betting on life to get better and your own ability to get yourself in a better position, always bet on yourself.

And that is why you should see every disruption as an opportunity. Without disruption, you do not get to make that bet. I always laugh at how insurance companies will call certain disasters "acts of God," but venture capital firms call chance success "serendipity" or "statistical luck factor" instead of "act of God." I believe we take life's turns, especially negative ones, too personally.

If any disruption has hurt you in the present moment or recent memory, you may assume it was meant to knock you off your feet. But that might only be the appearance of the situation. You have to look deeper. Don't judge a situation by its cover. It can bar hidden opportunities if only you have resolved to look for them.

~YOU'VE GOT TO BELIEVE~

Gold and cash are seen as precious resources, but belief is of even more value. It doesn't matter if you have a million dollars worth of gold if no human on the planet believes that it is real gold. The best part about belief is that it is a resource you can cultivate without spending money. You have got to believe in yourself first. And once you do that, your belief rises in value exponentially. And then you can believe in what you are doing and charge it with magnetic power. People are drawn towards confidence.

Belief has to be authentic in order to have its true effect. Those who do selfish things and try to accumulate wealth for the sake of accumulating wealth do not have access to the power of belief. Your life is a sacrifice; you must find what you can dedicate it to and do the work with such dedication that your belief in yourself is a byproduct of your belief in the mission. Most people wander through life without such purpose. And when they see someone super-charged with a sense of purpose, they rally behind him or her. You can be that person.

Every time you get something, you have to sacrifice another. That's just how life is. Even the most selfish person has to sacrifice a minute of time in order to experience that minute. We are either putting our life's time into something we believe in or into nothing. Why not sacrifice your time and effort for something that's worth the effort?

The human mind is amazing in that it has the capacity to unlock abilities one wasn't even conscious of. There are numerous cases of mothers lifting cars and other heavy objects to save their children. Whenever people are interviewed after such an event, they insist that they had no idea they could pull it off. This shows that we all have hidden abilities veiled by our own brains. With enough belief in your purpose and yourself, you can train your brain to go further.

Ever since my childhood, I thought I was going to be a great basketball player, and I never let my belief in myself falter. The confidence I had in my purpose and myself then overflowed into other areas of my life. And I want to bring that gift to you. I want you to give yourself the gift of belief.

~DON'T CONTROL WHAT YOU CANNOT~

There are two types of people: those who worry about everything and those who do something about a worrisome situation. And these categories rarely overlap because worriers are too busy being paralyzed by their stress. On the surface, the idea of not trying to control what one can't control seems like giving up. In reality, it is quite the opposite: by not trying to control what you cannot control, you can shift your focus towards controlling what you can.

This builds upon the tools presented in previous chapters. By believing in yourself, you can afford to be patient. And by being patient, you can be calm and calculated in your decisions. There are only two modes of being: acting or reacting. If you get swept up in emotions, you will react to external factors, but if you remain collected, you can make others react the way you want them to.

One thing that many people fail to grasp is the concept of seasons in life. You have your ups and your downs. There will be peaks and valleys in the story of your life, and if things outside your control look bad, you have to accept reality for what it is and focus on what you can control. It isn't your responsibility to make everything alright, but it surely is your responsibility to do the best you can with what you have.

If you find yourself thinking a lot about what's wrong with the world, you may be distracting yourself from personal responsibility. By complaining about what you cannot control, you trick yourself into believing that you're taking action. Do you remember the earlier portion regarding telling your friends instead of being a "Yes man"? Well, it is time I tell you something that might be hard to accept.

Complaining is not action. Showing concern is not action. Talking ill of politicians or business owners is not action. Action is action. Don't pat yourself on the back after displaying concern regarding things far away from your reach because you're doing that at the cost of making a difference close to home. The same time you spend worrying about a hundred things you can't control could be used to change one thing you can.

In conclusion, I want to remind you that millions of people worry about everything. If you skip worrying about the whole world's problems, the crowd of 7 billion won't miss you. Hundreds of people will worry about the economy, the stock market, the politicians, and other things. You could train yourself to look at things you control so you can do the best you can with what you have. I promise you that if everyone does the same thing, the world will be better off. So let's make the world a better place, one person at a time.

~THE GRIND~

There is no glamour in the grind. What most people fail to understand is that success happens at the goal-setting stage. So many individuals select goals that they like from afar. Millions of teenagers want to become famous basketball players, but they don't understand the grind required. I urge you to only pick the lane in which you can tolerate the grind.

I use the word tolerate because even in things that you love, there will be aspects that will bore you. The basics are often boring. I remember my first interaction with basketball. Working with my coach on the basics and spending hours getting them was the first step towards my success.

The business education industry is booming, with people claiming they can teach you a "Trick" to get it right. Here's the secret: there are no tricks that can replace the fundamentals. So what should you do? Don't go for a goal if you're not prepared to grind for it. Any goal you want to achieve via shortcuts isn't something you really want. There will be someone willing to do more for it, and that person will achieve it.

So don't ask yourself, "what can I do to get what I kind of want?" Instead, ask yourself, "What is it for which I will do anything?" And that "Anything" is not going to be some grand gesture. It will be hours of boring grind. If you cultivate enough belief in your purpose, though, you will be internally motivated to keep going.

Success comes at a price, and generally, you need to grind in order to become better than everyone else in that specific field. I could have said that life is easy and we all can have what we want, but that would be a lie. We can only have that for which we're willing to put in the work. Anyone who tells you otherwise is trying to sell you something.

Some people feel like their family name, or other factors can assist them. Certain things can help you get a little further, but nothing can help you replace the need for the grind. Let's take the example of Jeff Bezos. He is one of the richest men on the planet. He doesn't have as many Instagram followers as some of the top influencers. Why? Because he's not willing to grind for it. He has other things to focus on. If Jeff Bezos cannot get assisted by his wealth and connections when it comes to things he isn't willing to put effort into, how can you assume that you will have your friendships, family name, or money replace the fundamental need for the grind?

~NAYSAYERS~

Some people have Naysayer-phobia. The self-help industry has taken it for granted that Naysayers need to be eliminated from one's environment. Though there's some credibility in distancing yourself from toxic people, I love naysayers. I won't break bread with them every day, but I won't hide from them either. If anything, they motivate me because they push me to perform at the best possible level.

Your teachers and coaches can be among the first naysayers you will encounter. IF this happens, you have a choice: either accept whatever they say or take a stand. If you believe in yourself, you'll say, "I know myself better," and not take their opinions as your reality. Once you show them that you can do anything you put your mind to, they'll stop being naysayers.

That's when you should get yourself, new naysayers because if you don't have them, you're operating inside your comfort zone. Growth is a result of doing things you haven't previously done, and whenever you make a bold claim or set a worthy goal, some people will have reservations. But their stance against you is what ignites the necessary spark required to motivate you to do more and to be more.

That said, people can fall into the trap of trying to do things to prove their haters wrong. I don't like that idea because it places one's own happiness in someone else's hands. Instead of saying, "I will do this because you said I couldn't," you should say, "I will do this because I want to, even though you don't think I can't." There's a subtle difference between the two stances, but one is centered around your desires, and the other is around your insecurity. You must take the spark and make it serve you, or you will spend your life chasing approval.

Finally, there is the very real issue of being one's own naysayer. This is the toughest one to overcome because you can't access self-belief as long as you doubt yourself. And you can only fight naysayers with self-belief. The best way to get over this barrier is to simply pick smaller goals first and dominate them.

Once you realize that you're a conqueror who achieves everything he sets his mind to, you will start feeling more confident even with greater goals. In other words, if you work a minimum wage job and want to become a billionaire, set your first milestone as something you have an easier time believing you can achieve. Once you hit that milestone, set a higher target. Your vision can be as grand as you want it to be, but your next goal should be something you believe you can achieve. And that belief will keep you from giving up no matter how many naysayers surround you.

~BE YOU~

When you move in this reality, people build a perception of you. This view is usually airbrushed with wishful thinking. We are all somewhat guilty of this. People often recall red flags in hindsight but upon first meeting, see people the way they want them to be. What does that mean for you? It means that people will often want you to live up to the image of you they have created. You do not have the duty to live up to that if it doesn't align with your interests.

For better or worse, these images can be privileged or dis-empowering and have a lot to do with one's skin color, height, build, etc. Most of these factors are out of our control. As discussed in earlier chapters, you should not try to control that which is out of your control.

So what should you do? In my estimation, the best mode of being is to be oneself. Simply be who you are and stay true to your core identity. This will result in immense self-respect. Most lack of self-respect is a result of people being aware of their own hypocrisy.

When you act the way people want you to act, you lose your own respect. But when you stand by what you believe in, you can stand with your head high even if you take a temporary loss.

One key reason you should be yourself is that you have unique gifts and talents. To try to be someone else is to reject those gifts. Imagine Michael Jordan trying to be an accountant. There is no way he would put in the same dedication to a job he didn't want as he put into the sport he loved. Being yourself doesn't mean you have to reinvent the wheel. Jordan followed the same basics as the greats before him. I didn't try to invent new basics in my own basketball practice. It is advisable to follow others in order to be a leader, but you should do so constructively and with an open mind.

Napoleon was one of the greatest strategists of his time and crafted a new form of battleground leadership. Still, he built upon fundamentals of guerrilla warfare that existed, albeit on a smaller scale in remote regions. All in all, the game of life is all about making the most of the gifts unique to you while taking guidance from those who have excelled before you. To follow those who have done it before you without losing yourself in their approach is what it is all about.

~USE YOUR TIME WISELY~

At the time of the writing of this book, many people are in the COVID-19 lock-downs with plenty of "free time." You may be reading this later on, but you, too, will have loads of idle time at some point in your life. Therefore this lesson is a timeless one and must be followed regardless.

There is no such thing as free time. Every minute that you spend is subtracted from your total lifespan. So you have to be wise about how you spend your time. Spending time in leisurely activities isn't necessarily bad, but there must be a balance. Periods like the COVID lock-downs might make it seem okay to waste one's time. You have to be especially cautious of such times as you can get trapped in the time wastage loop.

A time wastage loop is where you waste time and feel guilty. But because you've already wasted an hour, you say, "now the day is ruined, let me just chill." And you take the whole day off. I have created a personal rule that always helps: no day should go by without learning something. This ensures that I never waste a day of my life without growing.

Whether this chapter changes or your life or becomes just another page you thumbed through depends on what you do with the guidance I provide. I recommend that you take out a pen and a paper right now and write down five things you always wanted to learn. These could be piano lessons you never made time for or a specific dish you loved but didn't know where to begin. Next time you find yourself doing nothing, simply look at that slip and take one of the items and learn how to do it online.

It is incredible how many opportunities are out there in the online learning space. From things like ATS university to Masterclass.com, there are tons of opportunities available for people to learn. If you are the type of person who likes to read, then you already know that books are a great way to expand your horizons.

Finally, I want to caution you against becoming an armchair expert. You need to get up and put into action whatever you're learning. In fact, I would advise you to get experiential about your learning. Start practicing things so you develop real-world expertise around them. You never know when your experience can turn into an opportunity.

~STEP OUT OF YOUR COMFORT ZONE~

In this chapter, I am not teaching you anything; I am just reminding you of something you have always known. If you had always stayed in your comfort zone, you would be a very large baby. You would not know how to speak or stand. And you would not know how to read this book. But you ventured into unfamiliar territories till they became familiar. Today, walking and speaking are things you don't even consider "skills" because they're that second nature to you. Wouldn't it be great if excellence was second nature to you?

I believe you can get there if only you return to your childlike curiosity. Learning is important, and I've stated as much in the earlier chapter, but there's a difference between forcing oneself to learn and having natural curiosity. When your curiosity overpowers your hesitation, you get out of your comfort zone. And that's the place where I want you to be.

Once you start living on the edge of your comfort zone, it will keep expanding as you keep trying new things and making them "normal." Outsiders who don't see all the effort that goes into this will often wonder how you're able to do things that they can't dare to try. The secret is simply stepping out of one's comfort zone one tiny step at a time.

You don't know how far you can go until you give things a try. There's no real way to find out. You cannot conduct research into your abilities while sitting on your couch, so quit unproductive armchair analysis and just do it. The samurai in ancient times had a practice of tightening their stomachs and charging forward. It was simply an act of acknowledging that there will always be hesitation no matter how seasoned the warrior. What's the solution? Don't try to unpack the hesitation. There's no use in analyzing it. Tighten your stomach and charge!

This starts in the morning. Stuff yourself with all the self-belief and positivity you can use so that you take the first opportunity you get to be out of your comfort zone. Once you observe yourself taking such chances, you feel more confident and keep conquering your hesitation throughout the day. When you go to bed, you catch yourself smiling because you know you outdid yourself throughout the day despite people's negativity. So remember that it is your duty to compel yourself to do different things and avoid the trap of moving in circles.

~STEPPING OUT OF YOUR COMFORT ZONE~

The previous chapter lays the foundation for my philosophy regarding comfort zones and how one can expand them. In this chapter, we will explore the tactics and the mindset you can use to dominate your hesitation with weaponized curiosity and hunger for excellence. Comfort is the enemy. Most people are tied to the patterns in which they operate. But patterns, by definition, keep us complacent.

There are looping patterns, and there are direction-bound patterns. Looping patterns are ones where you stay in the same place doing the same things. A toxic relationship that involves the same arguments over and over is an example of a looping pattern. A direction-bound pattern is one where you are headed up or down while following a predictable set of actions. A drug-addict is doing the same things over and over, but his life starts going in a downward spiral. Similarly, a business owner might be doing the same things repeatedly but will find himself headed upwards.

Analyze your life to figure out your patterns. Anything you've done every day is part of a larger pattern. Put all your repetitive actions on paper and note which ones are looping patterns and which ones are direction-bound. Differentiate the patterns that are taking you up (working) and the ones that aren't working. Remember that life is competition. Anything worthy of achieving or accumulating is going to attract competition. A goal that no one else wants is not valuable.

And if you want to achieve valuable goals, you will find yourself competing with others. Your competitors will know the set ways in which you will react. By moving out of your comfort zone, you will throw them off. You need to switch up your patterns not only to remove what's not working but also to keep others from imitating you or strategizing around your predictability.

Finally, you must realize that currency isn't currency. Attention is currency. The stock that has all eyes on it has immense value. The stock that no one pays attention to gets devalued into oblivion. This is true of humans as well. When you do unpredictable things, people are left with no choice but to listen. This again is a great tactic to use in your success strategy, especially when you find yourself struggling to get exposure. People need to overcome their shyness in order to get the appropriate exposure. And to do this, they must conquer the boundaries of their comfort zone.

~GET READY~

Have you ever heard the saying "getting ready is half the battle"? Well, that certainly is true for most things. Even when you cook something, the first step is to prepare the ingredients. When you have the right items, and you start the cooking process, things go well. Sometimes, despite your preparation, things start going wrong, and you have to improvise to bring the process back on track.

Similarly, in life, you must get ready even though you have the ability to improvise. People often believe that just because they may need to improvise in a certain area, they can skip the planning stage altogether. That would be the equivalent of saying you don't need to know the ingredients of cooking because you once made a dish while some ingredients were missing.

Flexibility and improvisation should be in your backup arsenal but should never be the number one thing you lean on. So how can you get ready for your journey? Start with your mindset. Get mentally prepared for the blessings you seek. So many people have an internal block: they don't believe they're worthy of the goals they're after. As a result, they constantly self-sabotage.

Aside from mindset, you should be ready for distractions. Have a game-plan to fight distractions and even make a list of apps and other things that can keep you from diluting your focus. Having an accountability partner can help. Whether it is a coach you get regular check-in calls from or a friend you look up to, you can have them as your guiding light whenever you begin to lose steam.

I would not have the same basketball experience without my coach. So coaching is one of the essential parts of getting ready. Determine how you will receive both guidance and accountability. If you can get professional coaching, you will get both education and accountability in the same person.

But if you can't afford a coach, you'll need to find the right learning resources and then sit with a friend to make an accountability pact. Of course, you will also need to remain internally motivated, but we will explore that in a chapter dedicated to focusing.

For now, you should remember that you can never skip the stage of getting ready. Even though spontaneity has its place, you cannot let it be your plan A. And when it comes to getting ready, you must be mentally prepared first.

~STAY FOCUSED~

The romanticized getting knocked down ten times to get back up the eleventh time is just a dramatized version of staying focused. It simply means that the one who keeps his eyes on the prize the longest wins. So the game of life is the game of staying focused. In his book The one thing, Gari Keller recommends that you tackle one thing at a time.

In my life, too, I have found this to be true. Of course, I handle multiple things, but whenever I take on a new project, I handle one massive challenge at a time. Your energy scattered in nine different projects will not get you anywhere, but the same energy laser-focused on one thing will bring exceptional results. I know this from my basketball practice. When I started, I tried to do too much too quickly and found myself frustrated by lack of progress. Once I picked a handful of basics and accepted the grind, everything changed. I was making one basic move at a time and, with sheer repetition, mastered my basics like none of my peers. Soon, I was turning heads with my game. I brought this same attitude to life outside. Results followed.

Cal Newport has an incredible book titled "Deep Work," where he expands upon this idea. The more focus you put into your work, the farther you can go. But if you let email, social media, and even your spouse distract you, you will later be resentful for all of those. Instead, dedicate time blocks to the grind. Do the work and keep your eyes on the prize. One of the ways people find themselves getting distracted is by over-thinking the results.

This is quite sinister as the subject is confident that he is "Working," but in reality, he is engaged in day-dreaming about results. Anything that distracts you from the necessary grind is not productive. And you can't bet on your willpower to get you through it all.

So change your environment to facilitate focus. One of the biggest challenges people had working from home during the COVID lock-downs was that of an environmental shift. Because people were unable to get into their working head space, they couldn't work with as much ease. But soon, most higher-level employees turned rooms within their homes into offices. As a result, they were more productive than they were at their offices. Why? Because the offices were designed by the company, but their own home-offices were designed personally to aid in focus. If that doesn't convince you to prioritize focus, I do not know what will.

~STAYING FOCUSED~

No matter what life throws at you, you have to stay focused. You will find a lot of things getting in your way whenever you're near a breakthrough. So if you feel like giving in to the distractions, you can take it as a sign that you're close to winning. Use that as internal motivation to keep going because the last thing you want is to lose momentum.

Staying focused will bless you with momentum. Remember how in school the most number of girls wanted to go out with the same guy? And how almost all the guys had a collective crush on the same girl? That isn't because either one was particularly the most attractive; it was just the result of momentum. It plays out in life outside of school. The same actors get the most roles, and the same business leaders get the most coverage. When you win, you keep winning more easily. But if you get distracted, you can fall off.

But those are problems for the later stage. Distractions don't wait till you're building momentum; they come even at the planning stage and try to solidify your inertia. What is inertia? It is the weight that keeps you where you are. It is the opposite of momentum in a way. The laziness that keeps you in your bed as you hit the snooze button is inertia.

That inertia is going to be easy to overcome if you finish planning and start acting. But during the planning stage, your mind will realize a million things that need to be done. Stay focused! There is an element of ego that gets manipulated by our surroundings. Even if you weren't where you are, the world would keep going, so stop worrying about the face pace of things around you. Keep your eyes on one thing that you control and can go for with all you have.

Finally, returning to my point regarding coaches and friends, the inverse also applies. Just like accountability partners can keep you focused, those who relieve you of your responsibilities can make it seem like it is okay to be distracted. I believe it is crucial that you remove such distractions from your environment. Yes, humans can be a source of distraction, and if you can't manage your social circle, you cannot engineer focus into your life. All in all, staying focused is about deciding that everything that isn't your problem, isn't your problem.

~IS ADVERSITY NEEDED?~

You must be cautious of the calmness because it can mean one of two things: you're going nowhere, or you're gearing up for a storm. Either way, you should not let things be when everything seems fine for an extended period. Consider what I stated about life's seasons. We know that there's always a dip after a peak, and if you seem to be on a plateau, the chances are that things are going wrong but haven't reached your detector. The housing bubble, the dot com bust, and so many other examples indicate that whenever everything seems "good" for a long period, we're in for a massive correction.

Some people believe that this only extends to financial markets, but even in social and political arenas of life, things being too good for too long is a sign of trouble. In hindsight, it seems laughable that as Obama made history becoming the first-ever black leader of the free world, some of us thought that the racial division and discrimination were coming to an end. And we all know what happened the following election cycle.

Now that we've established the fact that things being "fine" for too long can be a sign of a storm, what should we do? We should welcome adversity. Adversity is a great teacher. If everything went right, you wouldn't learn anything. I often say that one has to fall and even hit their head on the curb a few times in order to learn how to ride a bike. If something as fundamental as riding a bike requires trouble, how can you learn the more important lessons of life without trouble?

You have to remember that at no level in life are you immune to this principle. Even presidents learn from first-time crises. COVID-19 is a great example of the people who supposedly know what they are doing finding out how wrong they were. Initially, no one thought that the corona-virus could transfer from human to human. And you know where we are.

But there's no way we will go through the same thing a second time. Why? Because adversity has strengthened us and made us faster. That's why you should not have a phobia of adversity. If you're afraid of trouble, your subconscious will tune it out of your focus, and you'll not realize how much trouble you're in till it is too late. So keep an eye out for trouble, and instead of getting scared, get excited when you spot it.

~OVERCOMING ADVERSITY~

There's a saying that asserts that whatever doesn't kill you makes you stronger. I don't like that this phrase puts the burden of not killing you on the external factors. I discussed how important it is to focus on what you can control. Therefore I rephrase this as "whenever you overcome adversity, you become stronger." This places on your shoulders the responsibility of beating your problems into submission.

The biggest challenge most people face is timing their problems. Adversity often springs upon us when it is least expected. And the best way to beat it into submission is to first smile at it. If you show fear, it will overpower you completely. This way, the universe knows that you can't be crushed. You can handle anything it throws at you. You always come out stronger on the other end.

With each adversity you overcome, your belief in yourself grows stronger. This is a great thing, especially if you come out on the other end with better capabilities. Another great thing about adversity is that it brings opportunities. If all opportunities were apparent, then they would have been availed already.

The greatest opportunities are always hidden. And those too afraid to look miss out on them. When you smile and remain collected during a crisis, you unlock access to hidden opportunities. The questions you ask bring you the answers that create your reality. Most people instinctively ask themselves, "how can I escape this?" instead of "how can I use this to my advantage?"

It is quite difficult to believe for most people, but you can actually come out on the other end thankful for the fact that you went through the difficult time. Why? Because you're better off for it. If this doesn't convince you that welcoming adversity with an eye for opportunity is ideal, then let me remind you that you have no other option.

You don't get to opt out of adversity in life. It is a reality of life, and you may turn a blind eye to it, but everyone goes through difficult times. If you hide your head in the sand, you're perpetuating the culture of being a victim of reality. But if you smile in the face of adversity, it spreads throughout the universe and turns the tide. People facing adversity elsewhere may also smile because you chose to do so too. Ultimately it is the question of who you are. Are you someone who makes the most of what he or she has? If so, welcome adversity.

~OPEN YOUR GIFT~

Life is the first gift we receive, and so many people lose it while they're physically alive. Many are spiritually dead because they deny themselves access to their internal gift. Most don't even know that they have unique gifts because they're too afraid to accept them. It is like a superpower. Once you accept that you have the ability to do more, it becomes your responsibility to do more.

God gave you your gift before you were born, something that partnered with the gift of life. And only by realizing that you have this gift can you bring life into your "living." So how can you realize this gift? Firstly, you have to let go of people's opinion of what you're good at. People have a very blunt and narrow view of what others can be good at. That's why they always ask the tallest guy in the room if he tried basketball. Don't rely on people's opinions of what you're good at.

Focus on what feels good. What do you enjoy doing and appreciate on the inside? You may say, "but Reginald, what feels good to me doesn't make money!" While finances are important, your gift doesn't necessarily need to be immediately monetizable. In fact, your gift could be something as abstract as how much you care about people. Never deny your gift because it doesn't make money.

You can have more than one gift. That's why I encourage self-reflection. Do not skip your gifts because you believe they are unimportant. It doesn't matter how many gifts you have if you fail to acknowledge them. So please pay attention to every single gift. Feel free to write them down so they're in front of you and you can maximize each one's potential.

    Finally, I cannot emphasize enough the importance of isolated reflection. You may be surrounded by people who keep telling you that you're more gifted in one area because of their own interests or biases. In reality, your time might be better spent exercising a different gift. In life, the troubles you face will almost always require you to lean into your gifts. If you deny yourself the tools you need to overcome difficulties, you'll find yourself trapped. IF you feel trapped right now, chances are you have not acknowledged your gifts. Figure out what it is that you're good at, and you'll find out how you can defeat your problems.

~OVERCOMING THE ODDS~

Quitting becomes a habit. If you quit once in life, you'll want to quit every time things get tough. It doesn't matter how many times you've quit before; if you quit now, you'll perpetuate the cycle, but if you take a stand, things might be tough, but with enough self-belief, you'll overcome the odds. The difference between quitting and persisting is that of dreaming. If a failure gets you to quit dreaming, then that's the end of everything. However, if you continue dreaming, you have the ability to get back up, no matter how many times life knocks you down.

You can either get conquered by your fears, doubts, and obstacles or conquer them. It all depends on what you think of yourself. No matter how able you are, if you believe you can't do it, you won't do it. On the other hand, believing you can overcome the odds will lead you to victory. You will realize things about yourself that you previously didn't know.

Most often, the obstacles in your way aren't even physical. They could be psychological. You may need to overcome the way you were programmed to think. You may also need to overcome people pointing fingers at you and laughing. There's plenty of judgment around anyone who dares to stray from conventions. And success never comes from doing what everyone else is doing.

Do not spend too much energy battling judgments, convincing naysayers, or trying to explain yourself to others. You'll need this energy to fight your battles. Pick your battles and skip the ones that don't matter. The easiest way to overcome others' judgment is by not caring what they think. By continuously pursuing your dream regardless of the odds, you can completely change your life.

Most people don't even try their best. That's because they reserve their best shot for perfect conditions. Life never gives you the perfect conditions. So approach your journey with the following philosophy: your best shot cannot be conditional. You have to try your best regardless of the circumstances.

Sometimes you might feel backed into a corner. For true dreamers, this can serve as the fuel they need to fight. It can be the perfect way to get one out of their shell. The odds can turn in your favor once you apply enthusiasm and action to your passion. But if you keep waiting for the right time, it will never come.

~DON'T LIE TO YOURSELF~

You cannot get manipulated by honesty. People often have to lie to themselves to talk themselves out of their own dreams. That's why I stand by the sentiment that "the thing you are afraid of is who you are." And you can either own that or let it own you. So you should first be honest about what you're afraid of.

Once you're honest about that, you can access the ability to get rid of the fear that is stopping you. Doing so will help you become your own creator. You will have the resources and the daring to create your own reality. If you don't, you'll look for someone else to come around and make your dreams come true. So it is your choice: what do you want to do? Do you want to acknowledge the creator who lives inside you or be a hopeless dreamer waiting for the world to hand you your dreams on a silver platter?

Fear is the natural reaction of aiming for something outside one's comfort zone. In a previous chapter, I emphasized the need for one to overcome the boundaries of their comfort zone. You shouldn't be ashamed to have some level of fear. However, acknowledging fear and holding onto fear are two different things.

Acknowledging is important as it helps you avoid denial. You can't overcome fear if you deny that you are afraid. But once you acknowledge it, you must decide to let it go so you can move into action. Once you're in the middle of the thing you were previously scared to do, you'll notice all your fear disappear instantly. That's because your brain realizes that there's no utility to keeping you scared; you've already done that which it was terrified of.

Fear can get you so internally focused that you miss out on the bigger picture, so please do yourself the favor of hitting pause on fear, and you'll find golden opportunities in the adversities of life. Consider your fear as the lamb you need to sacrifice to get anything worthy in life. The person who wins is the one with the most control of the game. But you cannot control the game if you can't control yourself. Take hold of your emotions and become the decision maker. When fear becomes optional, you can decide not to be afraid. And when you have the power to decide that, you have all you need to be successful.

~EPILOGUE~

Congratulations on making it to the end of this book. It has been all about your success and how you can move through life with more control and take hold of your destiny. But while you're on that path, remember not to judge people by appearances. You do not know what life puts people through. Their appearances, apparent beliefs, and the shell that is social performance can all be a facade. By learning to look past it, you find allies where others see enemies and notice red flags where everyone sees green pastures. Needless to say that this is of exceptional value. Finally, remember to get back up. Life may put you through the wringer, but if you refuse to see yourself as the victim, the universe has no other option but to give you what you want.

~ABOUT THE AUTHOR~

www.ingramcontent.com/pod-product-compliance
Lightning Source LLC
LaVergne TN
LVHW030324070526
838199LV00069B/6558